First published in 1990 by
Bossiney Books,
St Teath, Bodmin, Cornwall.

Typeset and Printed by
Penwell Printers Ltd.,
Callington, Cornwall.

ISBN 0 948158 61 1

PLATE ACKNOWLEDGEMENTS

Front cover photography by
Ander Gunn
Back cover photography by
David Clarke

The Barnes Collection: page 63
Ray Bishop: pages 36, 56, 57
BBC Enterprises: pages 34, 78, 84
Central Independent Television: page 49
English China Clays: page 71
Ken Duxbury: page 87
Ander Gunn: page 45
HTV West: pages 24, 29
Richard Hawken: pages 21, 33
Leon Suddaby Gallery: pages 35, 40
The Penzance Library: page 41
Felicity Young: pages 19, 72

LOCATION — CORNWALL

David Clarke

BOSSINEY BOOKS

About the author
DAVID CLARKE

*Born in Wilmslow, Cheshire, David Clarke grew up in
Blackpool and was educated at Lytham St Annes. After
five years at art school, where he gained a National
Diploma in Design, he served a year in Cyprus as one of
the last National Servicemen. The next ten years were
spent teaching and lecturing in art in the north east of
England, South Wales and London, as well as contribut-
ing travel articles to magazines. He also spent two years
in the travel industry, working at the London headquarters of a leading tour operator.*

*David Clarke moved to Cornwall in 1971, working first
on a local newspaper and then on the county magazine
'Cornish Life'. He became its editor in 1974 and since
then has also written two travel guides and contributed
to several books about Cornwall, including 'The AA Book
of British Villages', 'Secret Britain', 'The Cadogan Guide
to Cornwall', and 'The AA Ordnance Survey Leisure
Guide: Cornwall'.*

*As an editor/journalist, he has covered the location
filming of most television and film series in Cornwall
over the past 16 years. A meeting with 'Poldark' author
Winston Graham led to him accompanying the film unit
to various locations during work on both series, and sub-
sequently to writing 'Poldark Country' in 1977 for
Bossiney Books.*

David Clarke

Why Cornwall?

'TREASURE Island', 'Love Story', 'The Eagle Has Landed', 'Dracula' and 'Straw Dogs' are just a few of the unlikely mix of films to be partly shot in Cornwall. Its beaches, coves, moors and villages have been used to represent the French coast, the West Indies, the Highlands of Scotland, Australia and Eastern Europe. It has also – mainly through the works of Daphne du Maurier and Winston Graham – been used to represent its own eighteenth and nineteenth-century self.

The special magic of Cornwall has been attracting holidaymakers since Victorian times. The peace, beauty and unspoilt coastline of this final tip of Britain has always acted as a magnet to people growing weary of industrial ugliness and suburban sprawl.

Jutting out into the Atlantic Ocean, Cornwall also enjoys some of the cleanest air in Britain. Just walk through any village in Cornwall and you will see rooftops covered with an orange coloured lichen – Xanthoria – which will only grow where the air is unpolluted. This pure air allows a clarity of light which has been likened to that of Greece. It attracted many famous artists to Cornwall in the 20s and 30s and inspired numerous early photographers to set up their tripods on clifftops and in fishing villages.

Cut off from the rest of Britain by its very geography, Cornwall has also largely managed to retain its own distinctive Celtic character, with its own music, sports and even its own language.

So when the first film-makers looked around for suitable outdoor locations, Cornwall quickly became a popular choice. The light was

Sherlock Holmes and Dr Watson, alias Jeremy Brett and Edward Hardwicke, dressed against a cold Lizard morning.

right; the weather was mild; the population was small enough not to encroach on filming, and the landscape, wooded estates, ancient green ways, small field patterns and old farm buildings looked much as they did centuries ago.

The great variety of scenery – ranging from wind-blasted moorland to peaceful, tree-lined creeks; from rugged, rock-strewn beaches and towering cliffs to semi-tropical gardens – also allowed Cornwall to stand in for many far-distant parts of the world. After all, why go to the expense of dragging a film unit half way round the world to the Caribbean when there is a suitable location at the end of the A30?

Add to this the plentiful availability of good accommodation for the often large film crews, the willingness of local people to enjoy and help with the film-making without getting in the way, and the sheer pleasure gained by actors and crew in staying in such a beautiful part of the world, and you can understand why Cornish locations have proved so popular. The film stars love coming down to Cornwall; in fact, many choose to live here when they are not working. They enjoy the relaxing atmosphere, far away from the pressures of the film and television industries.

As for the Cornish people themselves – they love it too. After all, where, in the past 50 years, could you have bumped into Laurence Olivier, Will Hay, Dustin Hoffman, The Goodies, Donald Sutherland and Robert Newton while strolling on the beach? Where else could you have met Sherlock Holmes, King Arthur and Dracula in the local pub, or watched a game of cricket between the Poldarks and the Warleggans?

I have only been able to deal with some of the films shot in Cornwall in this book and I realise there have been many others, as well as numerous documentaries and nature programmes, not to mention various episodes of 'Treasure Hunt' and 'Interceptor'.

But I hope that this guide will help the film and television fan to 'pin down' some real-life settings from a few favourite films. I also hope it will sometimes lead the reader away from the beaten track to enjoy some of the hidden and less-known areas of this beautiful country.

St Ann's in the 'Poldark' books was based on St Agnes where the delightful stepped row of miners' cottages, known as 'Stippy Stappy' leads to the village church.

8

'Going for a take'

S HERLOCK Holmes and Dr Watson stood in a small gulley
near the edge of the cliff. A thickening mist swept in from
Mount's Bay, almost obscuring the two figures. Holmes pointed to
a small mark on the rocky wall and Watson moved closer to

**The Granada Television crew, high on the desolate moorland
of West Penwith, prepare to get some Holmes and Watson
action 'in the can'.**

Local archaeologist Craig Weatherhill performing a seemingly impossible feat by lifting a granite stone to shoulder height. The polystyrene 'prop' now rests alongside his fireplace.

inspect it. He stepped back as a third figure approached, walking up to the detective and holding the end of a tape measure to his nose. He made a note on a piece of paper. 'We'd better go for a take now. The weather's closing in,' he said, moving away to a small group of people dressed in warm weatherproof clothing, huddled together on the desolate cliff top. The great detective threw aside a cigarette, did a little dance in a most un-Holmesian manner and said 'Come on then, lads. I'm dying for a hot pasty!'

Actors Jeremy Brett and Edward Hardwicke had been filming

since eight o-clock in the morning down on the beach at Kynance Cove. This was to be the final series of *'The Return of Sherlock Holmes'* made by Granada Television, and this first episode–*'The Devil's Foot'* – was being filmed in Cornwall over a two-week period in the spring of 1988.

The weather had been misty and wet, ideal for conveying the mysterious atmosphere and emptiness of Cornish moorland suggested in Conan Doyle's original story. But today, the mist was proving too dense. 'We're losing the light,' said the cameraman, aiming a light-meter at the sky. The director called to both actors: 'OK, Jeremy? OK, Edward? Let's shoot it. Quiet please! QUIET!'

A walkie-talkie crackled as the production manager asked his assistant on the road above to stop anyone walking into shot. 'Roll film' said the director and a clapperboard was clicked in front of the camera – ' "Devil's Foot". Scene 29. Take two'. Only the roar of the waves below could be heard as the director said '. . . and Action' and the two actors walked into shot.

In the final production, this scene would last just seven seconds, but it had occupied a small army of skilled technicians since dawn. In the gulley itself were the actors, the camera and sound recording team, make-up, costume, script and continuity girls, lighting technicians, production manager, producer and the director.

Thick electrical wires snaked across the gorse to the flat Lizard moorland above where cars, Range Rovers, a couple of large vans, a 40-seater coach and a generator were parked. A group of actors and extras, the production buyer, the props team, the designer and a National Trust warden stood by a small catering van eating pasties and sandwiches and drinking hot tea from plastic cups. Nobody seemed surprised that one actor, Norman Bowler, was dressed in a straitjacket. He was playing a madman who was about to be carried away in a horse-drawn van to the asylum.

Further along the track stood a horse box from which two large horses were led. One was steered between the shafts of a carriage

'It's a funny way to earn a living,' reflects actor Norman Bowler as he stands in the mist on the Lizard Peninsula dressed in a straitjacket. He was playing the role of a madman about to be driven away in a horse-drawn carriage.

Wearing a false beard and broad smile, actor Dennis Quilley tests a Cornish standing stone for authenticity. It was, in fact, another polystyrene model created by designer Michael Grimes.

The camera, mounted on a 'dolly' runs along its track, following Sherlock Holmes as he walks past Lanyon Quiot. The strange stone structure was erected as a chamber tomb in neolithic times.

which had been transformed by the designer, using gaffer tape and rolls of black stick-on plastic, into a suitably sinister-looking vehicle. The designer walked to an ancient, lichen-covered Celtic cross, picked it up and moved the polystyrene replica further along the track, where he used a spade to 'plant' it, ready for the next shot. 'It's a bit like a circus really,' said the production buyer, as he sat eating in his van surrounded by an assortment of guns, swords, potted plants, stuffed animals, harness and rolls of imitation grass. 'We roll into town – unload – perform the business and head off to the next location.'

As mist swirled across the flat Lizard Peninsula, the 50-or-so team gathered at the catering van and had a welcome break. A couple of coastal footpath walkers, suddenly coming upon Sherlock Holmes sitting on a boulder chewing a pasty, stared in amazement. He asked them if they thought the weather would

improve, but they were too dumbstruck to reply.

Normally, the crew would have headed for the warmth of the nearest pub to enjoy their lunch break, but in such a remote, cold and soggy spot as this, they were glad of the comfort and shelter provided by the mobile catering van. When filming near Cadgwith the day before, the local fishermen had been greatly amused to find Sherlock Holmes and Dr Watson, in costume, enjoying a lunchtime pint in the pub.

By midday the mist had cleared and it was decided to shoot a complex scene involving two horse-drawn carriages passing each other on a narrow muddy track. The camera was mounted on top of a car and followed the carriage bearing Holmes and Watson. The sound man also stood precariously on the car's roof, holding the sound boom over the actors as they trundled along the track.

All went well until the horse passed the polystyrene cross. In spite of the authenticity of the object, the horse seemed to sense its presence and shied away from it, ruining the shot. The vehicles slowly returned to their starting positions and they went for a second take . . . and a third . . . and a fourth. After a fifth disastrous attempt, the cross was removed from the roadside and the horse performed perfectly. However, the noise of an overhead jet plane meant a long pause before yet another take. It was nearing sunset before this ten-second scene was 'in the can' and the actors, technicians and crew made their way back to their Falmouth hotel and an early night. They were due to start work the next morning at 7.30, when the 'circus' would be appearing on the desolate heights of the West Penwith moors.

Sherlock Holmes (Jeremy Brett) in sombre mood as he paces the melancholy moor in search of an answer to another mystery.

King Arthur and Dracula

S TANDING on the rocky beach at Tintagel, looking up at the ancient ruins perched on the high headland and at the waterfall plunging over the slate cliffs, it is easy to see how this setting fuelled the legend of King Arthur. It inspired the poet Tennyson, and thousands of pilgrims who have visited the site since Victorian times.

Whether or not this was King Arthur's birthplace is open to

Ava Gardner and Robert Taylor, the stars of MGM's 'Knights of the Round Table' made at Tintagel in 1953. King Arthur has now grown into a thriving industry attracting thousands of visitors each year to the castle ruins on the cliffs.

debate. The ruins on the island, long thought to have been a Celtic monastery, are now thought to have been a chieftain's stronghold or a pre-Conquest trading settlement. The castle itself was built in the twelfth and thirteenth centuries.

Whatever the truth, the stark grandeur of Tintagel proved irresistable to MGM when in 1953, they filmed '*Knights of the Round Table*'. It was the company's first wide-screen film and a realistic and spectacular location was required for this story of the famous love triangle – so what better place than the original setting. The film was photographed by the brilliant Freddie Young, who made the most of the new technology and the superb scenery to portray King Arthur's Cornwall in all its wide-screen wonder.

The film starred Robert Taylor, Ava Gardner, Mel Ferrer, Stanley Baker and Felix Aylmer, all of whom stayed, appropriately enough, at the dramatically-sited King Arthur's Castle Hotel. Shot out of season to avoid attracting too much attention from visitors, the famous cast nevertheless drew 'Oohs!' and 'Aahs!' from the local people as they did a little sightseeing between filming. After all, it's not every day you see Ava Gardener buying a stamp in your local post office.

The King Arthur's Castle Hotel was no stranger to celebrity

King Arthur's Castle Hotel, standing proudly on the Tintagel clifftop, was a favourite with Sir Noel Coward, Ava Gardner, Robert Taylor and a host of other stars.

The slate ruins of Tintagel Castle, mainly date from the 13th Century, 700 years after King Arthur's time. The original castle was built in 1145 by Reginald, Earl of Cornwall.

guests. Back in the 30s and 40s, Noel Coward was a regular visitor. It was also the accommodation choice of the cast of the 1979 version of *Dracula*, directed by John Badham.

Bram Stoker's classic story required a suitably Gothic location, and the forbidding ruins, towering cliffs and rugged headlands of Tintagel, the crashing Atlantic waves and lowering skies, all helped add to the atmosphere.

Dracula was played by the American actor Frank Langella, and the cast also included Kate Nelligan, Trevor Eve and the great Donald Pleasance, making one of his many filming visits to Cornwall. The most notable name in the cast, however, was undoubtedly Sir Laurence Olivier, who played Doctor Van Helsing. He stayed at Tintagel in a separate, smaller hotel, and is said to have thoroughly enjoyed his trip to Cornwall, visiting old friends who lived locally and walking unnoticed through the streets of many small fishing villages.

One wonders whether Olivier visited Dame Daphne du Maurier at Kilmarth, for it was her novel, *Rebecca*, that gave him one of his greatest early, starring roles.

The great Olivier must have been suitably crestfallen when he met one local lady shopkeeper who misheard his name and thought he was the 1940s radio comedian Vic Oliver. 'He looked puzzled when he entered the shop and I told him how funny I thought he was and how much I admired his fiddle playing!' she recalls.

Malachi's Cove was a film made in the Tintagel area in the 1970s. It was based on Trollope's novel, published in the reign of Queen Victoria. Trollope, who combined authorship with high rank in the Post Office, captured some wonderful Cornish images in his writing, and the film makers did precisely the same, especially some savage seas at Trebarwith Strand. The film didn't make general release but did appear on our television screen in the summer of 1989. It contained some splendid filming of the North Cornwall locations, showing yet again how the dramatic coastline in particular can be used effectively on film. *Malachi's Cove* had an interesting cast, including Meg Owen, who went to star in the highly popular '*Upstairs Downstairs*' series on the small screen, Peter Vaughan, Donald Pleasance, Di Bradley and a young actress Veronica Quilligan. The film was directed by a member of the English aristocracy: Henry, Earl of Pembroke.

Lord Olivier, born in 1907, died 1989; a giant on the English stage and film set.

Du Maurier on film and TV

G IVEN Daphne du Maurier's lifelong obsession with her beloved Cornwall, surprisingly few of the film or television adaptations of her novels were actually filmed here.

In some cases film producers found it cheaper to recreate the settings in studios rather than send a film crew out on location. This

Mary Yelland (played by Jane Seymour) falls victim to the unwelcome attentions of Harry the Pedlar (Michael Goldie) in a scene from HTV West's version of 'Jamaica Inn'.

Hitchcock's stunning film, 'The Birds', was also based on a short story by Daphne du Maurier.

Jamaica Inn in the heart of Bodmin Moor and the familiar haunt of smugglers from Cornwall's north and south coasts in years gone by. Horse-drawn coaches used to speed past, fearful of what they might witness. Today, petrol-driven coaches stop to unload holidaymakers eager to soak up the atmosphere. The old slate-hung building inspired the young Daphne du Maurier's novel, though in her day the 'inn' was a Temperance Hotel. The inn as seen in Alfred Hitchcock's 1939 classic film was an idealised version of the real thing, built in the Hollywood studios.

also allowed the film designers to create rather idealised, romantic versions of how they imagined Cornwall to actually look. In other instances the original locations were switched to American settings, thus saving the American companies the expense of overseas filming, and aiming the end-product more directly at the US film-going public.

As a young lady, Daphne du Maurier stayed at Jamaica Inn, at the desolate centre of Bodmin Moor. Dating from 1547, the low, slate hung building was formerly the haunt of smugglers carrying contraband between the north and south coasts. But when Daphne du Maurier wrote her tale of Mary Yelland and the rascally landlord, Joss Merlyn, the building was in fact a Temperance Hotel, and the strongest beverage served was tea.

The 1939 film version of *Jamaica Inn* was directed by Alfred Hitchcock. It was his last British-made film before going to Hollywood, and it was the first of several adaptations of du Maurier stories. It was a great popular success, but there was much tampering with the plot and the author herself was less

The low-beamed interior of the real Jamaica Inn, now a comfortable bar and restaurant.

than pleased with the result. It starred Charles Laughton in a role greatly expanded from the original story, a dashing young Robert Newton and Maureen O'Hara. It was filmed almost entirely in the studio and had a very stagey feel about it. There was barely a Cornish accent to be heard and the film suggested that it was only a brief gallop on horseback from the Inn to either coast.

The story was remade in two parts for television by HTV West in 1983. Starring Jane Seymour, Patrick McGoohan, Billie Whitelaw and Peter Vaughan, it was once again heavy on studio mist sweeping across cardboard moorland and, while sticking more faithfully to the original story, the film visually bore only a slight resemblance to the original Cornish setting. This is because it was, in fact, partly filmed on Dartmoor. The designer did not feel that Bodmin Moor looked Cornish enough! Old farm buildings were re-

The turreted façade of Caerhays Castle, on the coast near Veryan, which represented Manderley in BBC Television's version of 'Rebecca'. Backed by dense woodland and beautiful gardens, the house is the work of John Nash, the architect of London's Marble Arch.

roofed and altered to represent Jamaica Inn and the result was certainly effective.

In Joss Merlyn's day, coaches sped past the inn, not daring to stop for fear of witnessing the dreadful goings-on inside. Today, coaches regularly draw up to allow large numbers of visitors to wander round the old inn and pause for refreshment. Surrounded by bleak moorland at Bolventor, alongside the busy A30, Jamaica Inn still retains much of its original atmosphere, with low oak beams, slate floors and smuggler's hidey holes.

The classic 1940 film of *Rebecca* was Hitchcock's second du Maurier adaptation. It provided perfect starring vehicles for Laurence Olivier and Joan Fontaine and was filmed entirely in Hollywood.

The real-life setting for *Rebecca* was the Menabilly estate on the eastern side of St Austell Bay, close to Fowey. And the model for the fictional Manderley was partly the large house called Menabilly, which, when the young Daphne du Maurier discovered it in the 30s, was romantically ivy-covered and rather neglected. The famous opening words of the novel, 'Last night I dreamt I went to Manderley again,' refer to the long private road leading to the estate from the nearby crossroads.

In 1943 Daphne du Maurier leased Menabilly from the Rashleigh family and lived in it herself. It was where she brought up three children and it was to play an important part in her life until she moved to nearby Kilmarth in 1967. The house is still a private residence and is not open to the public.

West of the house, the estate slopes down to Polridmouth Bay behind which lies a large lake and an attractive, small beach house. This beautiful stretch of coast, in the lee of Gribbin Head and only a short walk from Fowey, was the setting for a dramatic scene in the novel and the discovery of Rebecca's body in a wrecked ship.

The more recent BBC television production of *Rebecca*, starring Joanna David, is the only one of Daphne du Maurier's stories to actually be filmed in Cornwall. As a location for Manderley, they chose the delightful Caerhays Castle, the early nineteenth-century Gothic building designed by John Nash for the Trevanion family. Its dramatic, turreted facade and lush surrounding gardens provided the ideal setting for the fictional Manderley, and nearby

When HTV West filmed their 1983 version of 'Jamaica Inn' they converted old farm buildings into a replica of what the inn probably looked like in Joss Merlyn's time. But instead of Bodmin Moor, they filmed the location shots on Dartmoor.

Porthluney Cove was used for some of the filming. That same stretch of sand was also used for the filming of *Dangerous Exile* with Louis Jourdan in 1957, and several scenes of the second series of *Poldark*, filmed by BBC television. The castle is a private residence and is not open to the public, but it can be seen from the coast road.

Menabilly also inspired scenes in two other du Maurier novels. The first was *Frenchman's Creek*, filmed in California in 1944 and starring Joan Fontaine as a young lady who flees to her family home in Cornwall where she falls in love with a French pirate. The creek of the title is a long, winding inlet off the Helford River, over-

Film-making in Cornwall ... on location for the 'Poldark' series.

hung with trees and an air of haunted mystery. It is easy to see how this secret, eerie stretch of water sparked off the imagination of Daphne du Maurier. Frenchman's Creek is best seen from the water, but a footpath struggles along its southern bank towards the sea.

The second film inspired by Menabilly was *My Cousin Rachel*, filmed in Hollywood in 1952 and starring Richard Burton as Philip Ashley, a young man trying to discover if a mysterious lady, played by Olivia de Havilland, is innocent or guilty of the death of his cousin Ambrose in Italy.

The story was more recently re-filmed by BBC television, with Geraldine Chaplin in the title role.

Two further films adapted from stories by Daphne du Maurier, neither of which was filmed in Cornwall, were *The Birds* and *Don't Look Now*.

The first, a classic story of nature in revolt, was originally set in Cornwall, the theme being suggested when the author saw gulls and crows circling and swooping down on a farmer as he ploughed a field at Menabilly. When it was filmed by Alfred Hitchcock – his third du Maurier adaptation – in 1963, the location was changed to San Francisco and a nearby fishing community.

Don't Look Now, brilliantly filmed by Nicolas Roeg in 1973 and starring Donald Sutherland and Julie Christie, was based on a due Maurier short story and set in America and a wintry and atmospheric Venice.

But wherever they were filmed, the novels of Daphne du Maurier have created an enduring vision of Cornwall, for which we should all be grateful. As she pointed out in her book *Vanishing* Cornwall, the growth of industry, urban sprawl and tourism mean that Cornwall will change – and is changing fast.

The Penwith Peninsula – North From Land's End to the Lighthouse

NOWHERE is the atmosphere of Celtic Cornwall more potent than the stretch of coast from St Ives to Land's End. A switchback of a road winds, rises and dips between rugged cliffs and Iron-Age fields to the north and boulder-strewn moors to the south.

This landscape was probably seen to its best advantage in the

The famous signpost at Land's End and *(right)* **the raw, granite cliffs battered by Atlantic waves.**

BBC television productions of *Poldark* and *Penmarric* but the area has long been popular with film-makers.

The magnificent jagged granite spires at Land's End have inspired many writers, photographers and artists over the years. Battered by the full force of Atlantic storms, the high headland was known by the Romans as Belerion, or 'Seat of Storms'.

The Land's End State House Hotel, dramatically sited on the edge of the cliffs, was seen recently in the television film *The Shell Seekers*. The star, Angela Lansbury, not only stayed there during filming, but the character she played, Penelope Keating, also holidayed there, and in one scene enjoyed a meal with her grand-

Below: **Angela Lansbury waits patiently for filming to begin in an art gallery at St Ives during the making of 'The Shell Seekers'.**

Left: **Joss Ackland star of the BBC film 'First and Last'.**

daughter in the restaurant overlooking the crashing waves and the Longships lighthouse.

Being the most westerly point on mainland England, Land's End has also become a place of pilgrimage, and the start of many an epic journey to John o'Groats in Scotland. One such fictional adventure, filmed recently by the BBC, was *First and Last*, starring Joss Ackland.

This tragicomic drama by Michael Frayn tells the story of Alan Holly, a middle-aged man in poor health who, on his retirement from office life, decides to make one last grand gesture by walking the length of his homeland.

Filming was fraught with difficulties, including the death of the leading actor, Ray McAnally, half way through the film. He was

The State House at Land's End.

Robert Newton, leaning on a lobster pot, takes a breather with Belle Crystal and the director of 'Yellow Sands', on location by the harbour at Sennen in 1938.

replaced by an old friend, Joss Ackland, and all the location filming in Cornwall had to be repeated. Luckily the heatwave of 1989 lasted just long enough for this to be completed.

Joss Ackland is first seen taking photographs of the marvellous Land's End cliff scenery, the Longships lighthouse and the Seven Stones Reef, with the Wolf Rock light beyond, before being pictured himself by the world-famous signpost. He is next seen in a telephone box in Sennen Cove and walking past the wooden round house, which formerly contained a windlass used for hauling boats to safety during storms.

The Square in St Just, with the Pendeen Silver Band performing, was the next location before he is found walking on the golden crescent of sand at Carbis Bay and paddling, his shoes tied round his neck.

In a later sequence, the main character is seen buying a hamburger from a mobile cafe in pouring rain, watched by a coachload

Pendeen Silver Band in the square of St Just-in-Penwith where they appeared in the television film, 'First and Last', and another view of the square outside the King's Arms, St Just.

of elderly holidaymakers. This scene caused a few problems as, on both occasions it was filmed, the sky was cloudless. A group of 24 senior citizens from St Ives boarded a coach and were driven to a lay-by at Lelant. Ray McAnally – and later Joss Ackland – arrived, sweltering in heavy oilskins, and as the cameras rolled, false rain poured from a brilliant blue sky courtesy of special BBC rain-making equipment. The cheery pensionsers in the coach were persuaded to look suitably glum, and the shot was in the can.

When complimented on this effect, the BBC location manager put nature firmly in its place by saying they were also capable of making it look as though the sun was shining when it was really raining.

This same group of North Coast locations have also appeared in several other films and television series. The Goodies held their famous *Shootout at the OK Tea Rooms* in the streets of St Just,

Sennen, whose lifeboat station and wooden roundhouse were both featured in 'First and Last'. The roundhouse which used to house the windlass for hauling boats up the slipway, is now an art gallery.

Ready to roll ... members of the lighting, sound and camera crew used for the art gallery sequence in 'The Shell Seekers', which was filmed in St Ives.

Robert Newton walks on to a sandy stage at Sennen during the filming of 'Yellow Sands' in 1938.

and in an episode of Michael Palin's *Ripping Yarns* the beautiful stretch of coast near Cape Cornwall provided a background for 'Whinfrey's Last Case'.

Back in 1938 a film unit descended on Sennen to shoot *Yellow Sands*, (also known as 'Yellow Stockings') a romance based on a short story by Eden Phillpotts. The old fishing village, the broad beach of clean, white sand and the wild Atlantic waves provided just the right romantic feeling required by the director. The film starred the stage actress Marie Tempest, a young Robert Newton and that fine character actor Wilfrid Lawson. Both the latter were known for their drinking skills, and locals remember how they almost drank Sennen dry during the filming!

The narrow, bustling streets of 'Downalong' St Ives were most recently seen in the television film of *The Shell Seekers* when Penelope Keating, played by Angela Lansbury, paid a return visit to the town to relive old memories.

The sequence began with a panoramic view of the old fishing port from the Malakoff, before moving down into Fish Street,

Teetotal Street, The Digey and Salubrious Street, all loud with the cries of gulls and the distant crashing of surf on Porthmeor Beach. A wartime bombing scene was also shot among specially built ruins.

For one sequence, taking place in a St Ives art gallery, the 60-strong crew took over a local establishment to film the chance meeting of Angela Lansbury and the character played by Sam Wanamaker. When filming ended, the gallery owner, Leon Suddaby, had nothing but praise for the professionals of the team.

'They left the gallery exactly as they found it,' he said. Gallery assistant Jayne Jones, who was given a small walk-on part, was even more delighted when Angela Lansbury inscribed a copy of the book for her with the words 'To my co-star'.

As a young girl, author Virginia Woolf spent many happy holidays at a family house in St Ives. They inspired her to write her best-known novel *To The Lighthouse*, the central haunting image of which was the view across Hayle Estuary to Godrevy Lighthouse, built on a rocky island at the tip of the bay, near Gwithian.

When BBC television filmed the story in 1982, the producer tried to use as many of the original locations as possible. Scenes were shot on the beach and sandhills at Carbis Bay, Hayle and Lelant, a charming period house in the area and in nearby lanes and woods.

Several sequences involved arrivals and departures by train, and for this a special station was created alongside a level-crossing at Carbis Bay on the single-line railway which runs between St Erth and St Ives. A small station was built, and holidaymakers visiting St Ives by rail looked nonplussed as their train rattled straight past Carbis Halt without stopping.

As only diesel trains now run on this line, the effect of a departing steam train was conjured up by wafting clouds of white smoke at the actors on the platform.

Left: **Carbis Halt was constructed alongside the St Erth to St Ives line by a BBC designer for the film, 'The Lighthouse', based on the novel by Virginia Woolf. Cornish wrestling champion Jon Harvey (Camborne) starred along with Nicholas Geck and Michael Gough.**

The Penwith Peninsula – South
Love at the Minack
and Shell Seeking at Lamorna

F EW films have portrayed the beauty and grandeur of
Cornwall's coastline more effectively than 'Love Story' – not
the 1970 version with Ali McGraw and Ryan O'Neal, but the 1944
Gainsborough film starring Margaret Lockwood, Stewart Granger
and Patricia Roc.

It is the story of a dying concert pianist (Lockwood) who falls in

Patricia Roc *(left)* **and Margaret Lockwood, the stars of the 1944 film version of 'Love Story' shot in Cornwall.**

The magnificently-sited Minack Theatre at Porthcurno, the setting for some memorable scenes in 'Love Story'.

love with a young airman (Granger), who is himself going blind. This unashamedly romantic story and the superbly photographed scenery fed the need of a war-weary public for escapism and a breath of fresh air. The music, 'Cornish Rhapsody' by Hubert Bath, played on the soundtrack by the pianist Harriet Cohen, also became a firm family favourite throughout Britain.

The main setting for the film was the open-air Minack Theatre at Porthcurno, originally created by Miss Rowena Cade in 1923 and her life's work until her death in 1983. Similar in appearance to a Greek-style amphitheatre, it was created in a steep, natural basin in the cliffside and has a breathtaking natural backdrop of golden granite cliffs, white beaches and a turquoise sea.

Porthcurno Bay was also used for a memorable scene in the first

BBC television *Poldark* series when Demelza, pregnant with her first child, goes out fishing on her own in a small boat and begins to experience labour pains.

For the close-up shots the delightful Angharad Rees, suitably padded, was transferred to a small rowing boat from the 'Heather Armorel', a fishing boat which had been hired by the BBC and which contained all the camera and sound technicians. Although the sea was choppy, Angharad gamely rowed round the bay several times while the film crew, turning green round the gills, wallowed in the larger boat.

For the long shots, a 16-year-old crewman was dressed in Demelza's clothes and £250 wig to row round the bay a few more times. A BBC catering van had been set up on the beach, but the weather became so rough that when the film crew arrived back on dry land, they felt too ill to eat so the local boatmen, who had been watching, smiling, on the shore, took advantage of the unexpected hospitality.

A few miles inland from Porthcurno is the village of St Buryan, the setting for a very different type of film. *Straw Dogs* was an

St Buryan ... a peaceful village which became the scene of violence in the film 'Straw Dogs'.

From child star to international actress, Susan George has more than 30 major film credits to her name. In 'Straw Dogs' she played opposite Dustin Hoffman.

Angela Lansbury who played the role of Penelope Keating in the Cornish-filmed, 'The Shell Seekers', a Central Independent Television production for ITV network.

St Buryan Church.

altogether darker tale, made by director Sam Peckinpah in 1971, starring Dustin Hoffman, Susan George, David Warner and Peter Vaughan.

Hoffman played an American mathematician who settles with his wife in a remote Cornish village. They encounter first hostility, then irrational violence and brutality at the hands of the local villagers. The result is a cross between a Western and a horror film.

An empty shop in the centre of the village was transformed into an inn, with Peter Vaughan at his most menacing as the landlord, and David Warner played the village simpleton.

Despite the violent nature of the film, Dustin Hoffman seemed to thoroughly enjoy his stay in Cornwall, taking the opportunity to explore the coastal villages and soak up the atmosphere of Celtic Cornwall.

The idyllic wooded valley which runs east from St Buryan, straggles down between fields of early daffodils to reach the sea at Lamorna Cove. With its tiny pier and tumbled blocks of granite, this small cove has long attracted artists to live and work in the area. It also featured as one of the locations in *The Shell Seekers*, the television film based on the best-selling novel by Rosamunde Pilcher.

Filmed in the glorious summer of 1989 it starred Angela Lansbury, Anna Carteret, Patricia Hodge, Sam Wanamaker and Sophie Ward, the daughter of actor Simon Ward. Angela Lansbury played Penelope Keating, who returns to her Cotswold home where hangs a painting by her father of a Cornish beach. The filming at Lamorna was partly of flashback scenes to childhood holidays spent in Cornwall and also of a return visit by Penelope Keating.

Although the actors stayed at the Land's End State House during filming, the Lamorna Cove Hotel acted as production headquarters and the stars had trailers at the home of Lamorna Kerr, daughter of the famed artist J Lamorna Birch. Miss Lansbury, fresh from filming the *Murder She Wrote* series in America, had specially asked to be considered for the part after enjoying the novel. For Sophie Ward, this was also a return to a place where she had spent many happy childhood holidays. 'It's like coming to another country. So different and relaxing', she said.

The steep slipway of granite blocks at Porthgwarra, the tiny fish-

Porthgwarra, a tiny fishing community west of Porthcurno, was the setting for several episodes of the 'The Shell Seekers'. A steep slipway of massive boulders leads down to the water's edge. The holes in the rocks were drilled by miners to gain access to the neighbouring beach.

ing hamlet west of Porthcurno, formed an idyllic setting for several scenes in the film. In the background could be seen the entrance to a large tunnel, carved out of the rocky headland by local miners to join two small beaches, and also for smoking fish.

Filming for *The Shell Seekers* also took place on the sandy beach near Marazion, in a restaurant overlooking St Michael's Mount and across the peninsula at St Ives.

Holmes, Watson and the Mystery of the Standing Stones

HALFWAY across the Penwith Peninsula, on the high, bleak moorland, stand many mysterious stones placed there in prehistoric times. Holed stones, inscribed monoliths, standing stones and giant granite capstones perched precariously on upright stones are all that remain of chamber tombs, wayside markers and Iron Age hillforts.

When Sir Arthur Conan Doyle wrote his Sherlock Holmes story, *The Devil's Foot*, he had the exhausted detective and his associate, Dr Watson, visit Cornwall to rest and study these mysterious relics. The story itself is set on the Lizard Peninsula, but when Granada Television filmed the episode, they chose West Penwith as it is richer in prehistoric remains.

So it was that early one morning, with the mist barely cleared from the high moorland, the great detective and the good doctor took the winding road northwest from Penzance and then, along a narrow track, to the ruins of Ding Dong tin mine. From this high vantage point one can look across rolling moorland and ancient fields to both coasts, and by turn, the tall finger of the mine's chimney stack can be seen from far out to sea. But Holmes and Watson showed keener interest in snatching a hot drink from the catering van, one of eight large vehicles parked near the mine.

Filming was to take place at a group of standing stones at Boskednan, the remains of a Bronze Age round barrow some distance across the moor. To retain the atmosphere of the lonely, empty landscape, it was decided to leave the vans out of site and trek the final half mile, avoiding deep, peat-stained pools and hidden mine shafts. Only a thick electric cable snaking through the

Dr Watson (Edward Hardwicke) and Sherlock Holmes (Jeremy Brett), complete with an untypical balaclava, ride off into the Cornish mist.

dense heather linked the large film-crew to their source of power. The technicians and actors marched quite happily across the rough moorland until I told them how, only weeks before, a young walker carrying a rucksack had vanished down a mineshaft not far away and had lived for a week on a diet of toothpaste before being discovered!

The stones themselves are known as the Nine Maidens, one of several similarly-named groups of stones in Cornwall, said to be the remains of groups of young ladies who were turned to granite for dancing on the Sabbath. But for filming purposes, there was a problem. Only seven of the nine 'maidens' remained. Being sticklers for accuracy, Granada Television decided to add two replica stones. The designer, Michael Grimes, knows the area well and has a house in Cornwall. So he set local craftsmen to work in a garage at Gweek, carving standing stones out of polystyrene. Not just any old shape, but stones based on existing monoliths to be found in the surrounding landscape. These were then painted and roughened to form perfect lichen-coated copies and placed in the gaps in the circle of moorland stones. They were so convincing that several times actors were sent sprawling when they leaned against them and the 'maidens' toppled over.

For this sequence, Jeremy Brett and Edward Hardwicke as Holmes and Watson were joined by Dennis Quilley, playing an African explorer whom they meet while walking on the moors. The cold and damp of the morning was enlivened by the effervescent Quilley singing songs from musicals and operettas at the top of his fine voice, the sound sending rabbits and crows rushing for cover.

Jeremy Brett, the definitive Sherlock Holmes, caught in a pose uncharacteristic of the great detective.

Jeremy Brett was delighted with the location. He chatted to Craig Weatherhill, a local archaeologist, who had walked from his near-by home to watch, with amusement, the erecting of the fake 'maidens'. Craig explained how he rode his horse every day across this stretch of moorland. 'What I wouldn't give to live right here,' said Jeremy Brett. 'I've never seen a more magical place – so beautifully empty and clean and peaceful.'

After lunch the lights, tripods and cameras were dismantled and hauled downhill over rough moorland to Lanyon Quoit, the remains of a long barrow or chamber tomb alongside the Penzance to Morvah road. This famous neolithic monument comprises a massive granite capstone balanced on three upright stones. It is said that at one time a man on horseback could ride underneath it, but since it was toppled and re-erected in 1824, its height has been reduced.

Rails were set up alongside the Quoit so that the camera, mounted on a wheeled 'dolly', could follow Holmes in a 'tracking' shot as he examined the stones. A group of visitors to the site watched stunned as two of the crew marched towards them, each carrying a seven-foot-long standing stone on his shoulder. Lights were set up and Jeremy Brett stopped dancing between the stones and composed himself for a Holmesian exploration of the ancient monument. His performances of this character have rightly won Brett much praise, and he is arguably judged to be the finest Holmes of all time.

Filming over, the large crew of technicians and actors trudged with piles of equipment back over the moorland to Ding Dong Mine and the catering van. Craig Weatherhill walked off down the main road back to his house, delighted to have been given one of the replica 'maidens' to place by his fireside. Several cars almost ran off the road as their drivers saw him walking jauntily along, carrying a two-ton granite stone under his arm!

Horror and War in Mount's Bay

IN the year 1595, the tiny fishing village of Mousehole was invaded, sacked and all but destroyed by the Spanish Armada. One of the few remaining buildings was the Keigwin Arms, a manor house and later an inn, at the centre of the village.

In the intervening 400 years, Mousehole enjoyed a more peaceful

Mullion Harbour, or more correctly, Porth Mellon, which became a Russian port in 'Never Let Me Go', starring Clark Gable.

St Michael's Mount with its fairytale castle once acted as Dracula's castle for the television cameras. Access to the Mount at low tide is across a causeway.

existence. It built up a strong fishing fleet and, although this has now dwindled, the village remains one of the least spoilt in Cornwall.

In the past 40 years, however, it has been invaded several more times. I am not referring to the many tourists who visit this charming port, but to the large teams of film technicians and actors who have arrived, sometimes almost doubling the local pop-

Popular character actor Norman Mitchell prepares for a scene outside the butcher's shop at Mousehole, transformed into a general store for filming 'The Revenge of Billy the Kid'.

ulation overnight. Not that they are anything but welcome. The local villagers and fisherfolk generally treat it as a great compliment to their home port and don't even mind when asked to remove their television aerials or have their double-glazed windows replaced by authentic-looking replicas.

If you have watched any television series set in Cornwall, then you will almost certainly have caught a glimpse of the famous harbourside, with its buildings overhanging the water. The *Poldark* unit filmed here, as did those of *Penmarric*, *The Onedin Line* and countless others. Even a few well-remembered television commercials have utilised the charm and character of Mousehole's harbourside.

The most recent production filmed in the village was *The Revenge of Billy the Kid*, a comedy-horror spoof which has nothing to do with the Wild West, but a lot to do with a giant, man-eating goat. The feature film's £1 million budget is relatively small by modern standards, and the 30-strong crew of film technicians were mainly young professionals making their first film.

Although the unit was fairly small, their presence in the village was obvious. In the harbourside car park stood large vans of props and equipment and a throbbing generator, from which thick cables wound along the road and up into the narrow streets. Shop signs and window displays had been replaced, a waterside house had been transformed into a police station, sandwiches and cups of tea were dispensed from a table by the chapel, cobbled streets were lined with tripods, camera cases and cans of film, and several of the 'old salts' wandering the alleyways dressed in smocks and sea-boots were really actors or extras. It was all very confusing for a group of holidaymakers visiting Mousehole for the afternoon.

Although the film is not specifically set in Cornwall, the producer Tim Dennison explained why he had chosen Mousehole. 'We liked the close-knit community here, the atmosphere of the local pub and the narrow street. It has just the right claustrophobic feel to it'. This same close-knit feeling may well have inspired another fictional village, that of Llareggub, in Dylan Thomas famous play *Under Milk Wood*, for it was in Mousehole that he spent his honeymoon and lived for some time with Caitlin.

As the sun vanished behind the dense cloud, bright daylight was restored to Mousehole's narrow alleys by means of generator-fed lamps, ranged along the pavements. Bemused villagers stood around, arms folded with knowing smiles – they had seen it all before. And they knew their bid for stardom would come that evening when a scene for the film was to be shot in the Ship Inn, with the villagers acting as extras.

Facing the entrance to Mousehole harbour and standing in the centre of Mount's Bay is one of Cornwall's most-visited attractions – St Michael's Mount. This high pinnacle of rock rising from the water and topped by a fairytale castle presents a dramatic image. It would seem the perfect location for making romantic, horror or period films, but its familiarity has probably prevented its use in all but a handful of films.

In the fifth century St Michael the Archangel appeared to a group of fisherman on the southern side of the Mount. Edward the Confessor gave the Mount to the monks of Mont St Michel and it was they who built the priory on the summit. Henry IV turned it into a fortified garrison and it was later owned by a series of noble families, including the Bassets and, now, the St Aubyns.

The dramatic, soaring east wing was added in the 1870s and it was the medieval appearance of this section that suggested the Mount as a film location for the BBC television production of *Dracula*, shown in two parts, and starring Louis Jourdan and Susan Penhaligan. Seen in silhouette, with moonlit clouds racing past behind its turrets, the soaring image of St Michael's Mount sent chills up the spine.

When Anglia Television filmed *The Dame of Sark* back in the early 1970s, they decided to stick to the mainland rather than to take the large film unit to the Channel Islands, and to search for a similar harbour in Cornwall. They finally chose Porth Mellin, below Mullion village, on the east side of Mount's Bay.

Local boatmen and villages alike recall, with pleasure, the charm and friendliness of the film's star, the much-loved Celia Johnson. She played the Dame of Sark at the time of the German occupation of the Channel Islands, and local people, kitted out in Nazi uniforms, played German soldiers and officers. 'It was just like that classic episode of "Dad's Army" come to life,' recalls one extra. '...especially when during a break in filming we all went into the local pub – in uniform – for a drink. It's a good job it wasn't wartime!'

The fishing village of Mousehole, familiar as a film location for a number of productions and TV commercials.

Mullion's harbour has also appeared in several other films and television commercials – most recently the Peugeot car advert – but in had its most famous visitors during the filming of the 1953 film *Never Let Me Go*, when it represented a Russian port. The story concerned an American journalist, played by Clark Gable, trying to smuggle his ballerina-wife, Gene Tierney, out of Russia.

Laurie Francis remembers the visit by the stars to the Polurrian Hotel at Mullion. 'It caused quite a stir in the village,' he said. 'In fact, to prevent Clark Gable being pestered by the populace, we moved the head waiter out of his bungalow and allowed Mr Gable to stay there to give him a little peace. They all seemed to really enjoy it here and they loved the Cornish scenery and little coves. They also filmed in Newquay and Mevagissey.'

The Great Pola Negri Riot

O NE of the very first motion pictures to be filmed in Cornwall was the Gothic-sounding tale, *Street of Abandoned Children*, back in 1929. And quite a sensation it caused, too.

St Ives was the location, and the star of the film was Pola Negri, the exotic beauty of Polish aristocratic descent. This was a silent film, and when the unit arrived in St Ives with their large new electric cameras, tripods and lighting equipment, they were treated with some suspicion by the local folk.

We have a first-hand account of the events that followed in Pola Negri's autobiography:

'From the moment we arrived in St Ives, it rained constantly, holding up production for days on end . . . naturally the natives were very curious about us . . .' She felt that the 'natives' were overly suspicious and that they were 'certain that what was happening in their midst must be of satanic design and could well bring bad luck to all who came in contact with it . . .' Actors were rumoured to hold black masses and be practitioners of witchcraft.

'As a result it was initially very difficult for our production manager to persuade the locals to appear as extras, but raising the fees performed the miracle of lifting the curse of working for us.' Obviously no fools, these 'natives'.

Already famous for her romances with Rudolph Valentino and Charlie Chaplin, Pola Negri had just launched into a friendship with air-ace Commander Glen Kidston, who dashingly dashed down to St Ives in his little plane and startled the locals by landing in a nearby field. 'They were immediately convinced that God's

Exotic silent-film beauty, Pola Negri, who was responsible for 'unrest among the natives' in St Ives during the late 1920s.

wrath was descending from heaven for having permitted us to stay,' recalls Miss Negri.

As the appalling weather continued, so production ran even further behind schedule. When a Sunday morning dawned clear and bright it was decided to recommence working – even though it was the day of rest – a thing unheard of in those days in St Ives. Miss Negri takes up the tale:

'As we paraded through the village in our costumes, we could sense a certain strange hostility, and while the camera crew was setting up on the beach, we turned to find the local men bearing down upon us, armed primitively with pitchforks, rakes, spades, rocks and clubs. Their women and children marched behind ... we were frightened ...'

Luckily, the dashing Commander Kidston came to the rescue, and after 'discussing' the situation with the locals, it was decided not to film on a Sunday and the crew packed up and left.

As a postscript to this tale, it is interesting to note that when the film location unit moved on to work in Marseilles, they did not fare much better. They were filming in the port's notorious red-light district and had to work under constant police protection.

The finished silent film seems to have vanished without a trace, much to Miss Negri's despair. Another few months and sound equipment would have been available. 'We would have had the biggest hit in the history of English films.

Two views of St Ives at the turn of the century, with narrow cobbled lanes and, *left,* **its tidy harbour.**

The Eagle, The Onedins and Johnny Frenchman

THE South Coast harbour village of Mevagissey was one of Cornwall's leading pilchard ports in the eighteenth and nineteenth centuries. Within living memory more than 100 luggers packed into the harbour and the harbourside was lined with fishing stores, net-lofts and deep fish-salting pits. The narrow streets of colour-washed and slate-hung buildings and the old harbour walls provided the perfect location for the 1945 Ealing Studio

Tom Walls, who starred opposite Patricia Roc in 'Johnny Frenchman', a film telling the story of rivalry between Cornish and Breton fishermen which was made at Mevagissey. In addition to being an accomplished actor and producer, Walls, who assembled the famous Aldwych farce team, was also a keen sportsman. One of his horses won the Derby in 1932. This illustration was featured in the John Player album of cigarette cards depicting famous film stars.

The fishing port of Mevagissey on the south Cornish coast,
still a popular film location.

drama *Johnny Frenchman*, a tale of rivalry between the fishermen of Cornwall and Brittany.

The film starred Tom Walls, Patricia Roc and the French actress Françoise Rosay. Technical advisor during the 15-weeks of filming was a local man, Harry Mills. Now in his nineties, Mr Mills still has vivid memories of that time.

'I used to sit behind the camera with Mr Balcon and Mr Frend and point out anything that looked wrong. For instance, the story called for a catch of mullet to be unloaded, but the lads were unloading pilchards. In another part of the film, Madame Rosay was supposed to take a rope off a bollard and walk away, but she walked off with the bollard under her arm!

'Some of the local fishermen were called in as extras and given a few lines. One old boy was supposed to call to a group of fishermen, telling them to leave. He was supposed to shout "Aller! Tout suite!", but he forgot his lines and as the cameras rolled he shouted "Aller! . . .oh, bugger off!" '

Mr Mills also recalled the filming of the MGM drama *Never Let Me Go*, in which Mevagissey represented a Russian port.

'The best scene was where a car was being chased and it drove right off the end of the lighthouse quay into the water. That caused quite a stir! We got to know the stars quite well and I used to go drinking in the King's Arms with Clarke Gable. A very pleasant man.'

The little china-clay port of Charlestown, further up the coast, close to St Austell, is remarkable in several ways. Its existence is almost entirely due to one man, the industrialist Charles Rashleigh, who designed and built the port and village in just ten years, completing it in 1801.

China Clay was loaded on one side of the harbour while coal was unloaded on the other. This gave rise to two breeds of local men: those with clay-white faces and clothes, and those covered with black coal dust.

Although it is still a working port it has retained its unspoilt

The deep harbour of Charlestown, used as a location for many films and television series, was built in 1801 to handle china clay and is still a working port today.

charm and original buildings, and these have made it a popular location for making period films. The *Poldark* film unit made several visits, and many sequences of The *Onedin Line* were filmed in and around the harbour.

One of the reasons for Charlestown's popularity was the presence for many years of the old ketch the Marquesse which, converted into a three-masted vessel, provided an authentic background. George Warleggan and Ross Poldark argued and fought alongside it; various members of the Onedin family set sail on it; and it was also transformed into the Beagle for the filming of the BBC series *The Voyage of Charles Darwin*. Tragically, the old ship sank in the Caribbean several years later with the loss of many young lives.

Many location scenes for *The Eagle has Landed* were also shot here in 1976, when the small harbour was transformed into German-occupied Alderney in the Channel Islands. The story concerned a wartime German plot to kidnap Winston Churchill.

A German communications post was built at the harbour's edge, anti-aircraft guns were ranged along the beach, wooden steps led down to a U-boat and the Pier House Hotel was transformed into the George and Dragon pub, where a sign offered bed and breakfast for 5/6d.

The film's star-studded cast included Michael Caine, Donald Sutherland, Robert Duvall, Jenny Agutter, Donald Pleasance, Anthony Quayle and Judy Geeson. They stayed long enough to become part of village life and are remembered fondly by many of the local folk.

One such is Arthur Hosegood, a retired dental technician who lives on the harbour's edge.

'They were a very nice crowd,' he recalls. 'I got to know a few of them quite well. During the filming it was really strange to see German officers strutting about and racing about on motor-bikes and side-cars training their guns on the people. There was even a firing squad on the beach! It made you realise what it would have been like if we had been invaded.'

Like many others, Mr Hosegood was asked to remove his television aerial during filming, and he remembers with amusement when his house was painted twice – free of charge.

'A few years before, *Songs of Praise* came from Charlestown har-

Charlestown in the early 1900s.

bour and the BBC painted my house a brilliant white to act as a
background. For *The Eagle has Landed*, they wanted it to look
grimy and drab, like wartime, so they spattered it with mud and
dirty emulsion paint. They said it would wash off afterwards – but
it didn't. So the film people paid for it to be painted white again!'

The sandy beach and narrow streets of Looe were seen in the
dramatic television serial *Jumping the Queue*, starring Sheila
Hancock. One particularly amusing sequence featured a group of
local elderly people drinking in a pub in the town. As filming pro-
gressed and several scenes were shot and re-shot, so the extras
became more and more lively. Actress Jean Penhaligon, mother of
actress Susan, recalls how the whole sequence almost got out of
hand.

'Everybody began to sing and it got noisier and noisier. They
nearly had to stop filming, but Sheila Hancock seemed to enjoy it
and joined in with the fun.'

Long John and The Fal

T HE bustling port of Falmouth, the large expanse of water
known as Carrick Roads – the estuary of seven rivers and one
of the world's greatest natural harbours – and the deep water of
the River Fal have all provided ideal film locations over the years.

Perhaps most memorable was the 1950 Walt Disney version of
Robert Louis Stevenson's classic, *Treasure Island*, with Robert
Newton giving the definitive performance of that old rogue Long
John Silver. The cast also included young Bobby Driscoll as Jim
Hawkins, and a host of famous character actors, including Walter
Fitzgerald, Basil Sydney, Ralph Truman and Denis O'Dea.

A man who remembers the filming is Jack Snell, former cox of
Falmouth lifeboat. It was his job to tow the 'Hispanola' from its
anchorage in Falmouth's inner harbour to the various locations in
Carrick Roads and up the River Fal.

'She was a lovely vessel,' he recalls. 'She was really the Ryland, a
trading schooner, but she was converted into a pirate ship for the
film up at Bideford. They did a bit of filming up the Helford River,
but mostly they used the entrance to the River Fal, at Turnaware
Bar opposite Feock, and further up river near the King Harry
Ferry. I remember one day they discovered the battleships Ajax
and Achilles anchored there, and they had to be moved down river
so as not to appear in the shot.'

The wooded banks of the river and the lush growth of the sheltered Fal looked truly convincing as Treasure Island, but the palm
trees that appeared in almost every shot were in fact painted on

sheets of glass between the camera and the actors–a special effects trick dating back to the early days of filming.

Mr Snell was employed for the four months it took to film the location scenes, and he remembers the great attention to detail required by the director, Byron Haskin.

'We often had to shoot the same scene over and over again until it was absolutely perfect. They wanted one shot of the Hispanola turning at sea. She had engines and she could sail under her own steam, but we mostly towed her into position. The weather was all wrong, and it took over two weeks to get that particular shot'.

One amusing tale is told about Robert Newton during the shooting of the film. He is said to have dressed as an old tramp for a joke and gone into the Mexico Inn at Long Rock, Mount's Bay, for a lunchtime drink. The landlord took a dislike to his appearance, scowled at him and refused to serve him. That same evening Robert Newton reappeared at the inn, smartly dressed, and with all the actors. In loud Shakespearian tones he ordered drinks for the entire house, and then reverted to his tramp's voice to refuse the landlord a drink.

Jimmy Morrison, another Falmouth boatman, told me about the filming of *Dangerous Exile* in and around Falmouth harbour in 1957. It starred Louis Jourdan as a Frenchman who saves royalty from execution during the Revolution, aided by an English lass played by Belinda Lee.

'I was working on the film ship,' recalls Jimmy Morrison, 'and one day we were anchored off Carrick Point and it got rather choppy. Louis Jourdan sat on the foredeck all dressed up in his costume, waiting for filming to begin. But as the ship rolled from side to side he turned very green and had to be taken ashore.'

A lot of the film was made around Falmouth Bay and harbour, but mostly it was shot up the coast at Caerhays Castle. The main

The bustling centre of Falmouth today. The port's growth was largely due to the enthusiasm of Sir Walter Raleigh and the foresight of the local Killigrew family who had made money from piracy and privateering before they channelled their energies against the invading French and Spanish.

character landed on the beach there to get safe custody from the castle's owners.

Falmouth Docks have also been used by several film companies over the years – as Jimmy Morrison recalls:

'I recall Will Hay and Graham Moffat causing a lot of amusing havoc there back in the 40s, and also the filming of some scenes for *Scott of the Antarctic* in 1948. I was in my boat, the Mayflower, with all the flags flying as we filmed the departure of the Discovery, from the eastern breakwater, bound for the South Pole.'

The King Harry Ferry across the River Fal to the Roseland Peninsula. These deep waters and steep wooded banks were used during the filming of 'Treasure Island' by Walt Disney.

Clark Gable and The Beatles at Newquay

T HE arrival of Clark Gable, 'The World's Most Famous Film Star', in Newquay in 1953 caused such a storm of local interest that for much of the filming of *Never Let Me Go* he had to stay put in the Headland Hotel.

His co-star Gene Tierney also suffered from extreme public attention, as well as the attention of a thief, who made off with all her personal jewellery.

There was equal public clamour in the late 60s when the Beatles visited town. They were touring the country in a large bus filming *Magical Mystery Tour*, and Newquay's Atlantic Hotel acted as their base for some time, as well as the location for several scenes, including the famous ballroom scene, when the Fab Four descended the stairway all dressed in white and singing 'Your Mother Should Know'. Other scenes were shot on Towan Beach and at a nearby disued airfield.

Details of the filming had been kept a strict secret and for most of the time the film crew were able to keep one step ahead of the Beatles' fans.

The Headland Hotel, overlooking one of Europe's finest surfing beaches, has also acted as a base for several recent film and television productions. The television play *The Wild Things* was filmed in the hotel in 1988, as was *The Witches*, a childrens film produced by Jim Henson of Muppets fame. Starring Angelica Huston, Rowan Atkinson and Mai Zetterling, it is based on a Roald Dahl story and features a host of strange beasts created by Jim Henson's special effects team. Hotel guests were amused to find they were sharing the building with a group of little white mice

Jack Shepherd and Zoe Wanamaker as they appeared in 'Ball Trap at the Cote Sauvage', filmed at a tourist park near Newquay. Although set in Brittany, the Cornish coast, especially around Crantock, provided an authentic substitute.

and a bizarre witch's convention. The Headland Hotel's owner, John Armstrong, is a keen hot-air balloonist, and the film crew had hoped to use John's own balloon for some aerial filming. However, the wind was far too strong so they had to use the services of a helicopter instead.

The cast and crew of the BBC TV film *Ball Trap on the Cote Sauvage* also stayed at the Headland Hotel. For this gentle comedy, Cornwall represented Brittany, and a nearby tourist park was

Clark Gable, stayed in the head waiter's bungalow at Mullion.

transformed into a French camp-site. The film starred the magnetic Miranda Richardson as a free-spirited Frenchwoman who meets a holidaying English couple played by Jack Shepherd and Zoe Wanamaker.

Fistral Beach below the hotel was used as a location for some scenes, but most of the beach footage was shot at Crantock beach and the nearby sandhills. It must have been very confusing for holidaymakers to come across French road-signs, specially erected for the filming, and even more puzzling when they saw fields containing circles of white stones normally to be found in Brittany. Yes, they were polystyrene replicas once again.

Derelict tin-mine engine-houses and the scarred landscape of Jericho Valley and Blue Hills, near St Agnes, south of Newquay, provided the perfect eerie setting for the 1971 low-budget horror film *Crucible of Terror*. Former disc-jockey Mike Raven played a mad sculptor who turned his victims into bronze statues, but much of the film's atmosphere came from the beautifully photographed Cornish landscape.

North of Newquay and across the estuary of the River Camel, we enter Betjeman Country, and while none of the much-loved former Poet Laureate's work has been adapted as feature films, there have been many television documentaries featuring this area.

The beach at Polzeath was where John Betjeman enjoyed blissful summer holidays as a child, exploring caves and rockpools, and the surrounding countryside, with its varied coastline, villages, churches and tamarisk-bordered lanes, formed the subject matter of some of his most evocative poems.

Sir John lived in the charming village of Trebetherick, and his grave can be found nearby outside St Enodoc Church, whose small stumpy spire rises from a walled churchyard of tamarisks in the centre of a golf course and in the shadow of Brae Hill.

**The Beatles were the centre of attraction when their
'Magical Mystery Tour' film unit used Newquay's Atlantic
Hotel as its base.**

Poldark's Cornwall

I doubt if there are many corners of Cornwall not featured in one or another episode of BBC TV's *Poldark*. Altogether, 29 episodes were transmitted in two separate series, and although the interiors were recorded at the BBC's Pebble Mill studios in Birmingham, long sequences in every episode were filmed here in Cornwall.

Winston Graham's novels of life in late eighteenth century Cornwall, of the tin and copper mines and the rivalries between the Poldark and Warleggan families, caught the public imagination when they first appeared in print, and the television series, based on the books, have been firm favourites with viewers ever since. They have been seen world-wide and, thanks to Winston Graham's original vision, the Cornish landscape is now as familiar to viewers in Tasmania and Tahiti as to those in Tewkesbury or Todmorden.

When trying to track down the locations featured in the books and television series, one is faced with a problem. Most of the larger towns mentioned exist in reality: Truro, St Austell, Redruth, Looe, Falmouth and so on. But as these are all now large towns, cluttered with modern buildings and industry, the location hunters had to imagine how they would have looked 200 years ago. Luckily, Cornwall is rich in small inland and coastal villages where, give or take the odd television aerial or double yellow line, appearances have changed little over the years.

Thus, Falmouth was represented by both Mousehole and

Angharad Rees and Robin Ellis as Demelza and Ross Poldark leaving St Winnow Church, near Lostwithiel, after the wedding scene.

The Poldark cousins, Francis (Clive Francis) and Ross (Robin Ellis) ride through Trevellas Coombe, near St Agnes, past the remains of the Blue Hills mine.

Charlestown. In the former, the sixteenth century Keigwin Arms with its overhanging porch resting on stone pillars, provided a natural background, while the deep harbour and old wharves of Charlestown appeared as Falmouth in several later scenes. The episode when Ross first met Demelza at Redruth Fair was in fact filmed way up the north coast, alongside some old farm buildings near Portquin, and those wild smuggling sequences on the North Coast were mainly filmed in sheltered coves on the South Coast.

But, just as the events and characters in Winston Graham's *Poldark* novels are part real history and part fiction, so the settings are sometimes based on reality, sometimes they are composite pictures of several areas and sometimes they are pure invention.

The fishing village of Sawle and the nearby mining community of St Ann's, where much of the action takes place, are a case in point. They are partly based on the old mining village of St Agnes, only a few miles down the coast from Perranporth, where Winston Graham lived when he wrote the early *Poldark* novels. There is a delightful row of miners' cottages called the 'Stippy Stappy', just as described in the books, and the village is still surrounded by the remains of old mine-workings with names such as Wheal Kitty and Wheal Friendly. Study any old map of the area and you will discover that the village was in fact originally called St Ann.

Down a deep twisting valley watched over by more derelict engine houses, you come to Trevaunance Cove – very similar to the village of Sawle. Now a popular spot with summer visitors, this was once a small fishing village where the voices of fish-wives mingled with the sounds of horse's hooves on the steep cobbled street and the sea pounding on the shingle beach. It once had a small harbour, but this has long since been destroyed by ferocious Atlantic storms.

No *Poldark* filming was done in either place, but several scenes were shot in Trevellas Coombe, the long heather-sided valley east of St Agnes. The loudest sound you will now hear is the twittering of skylarks, but the valley once echoed to the roar and clatter of mining pumps and engines.

Nampara, the fictional home of Ross and Demelza Poldark, was situated high on the north coast cliffs above a small cove. The name refers to an area on the outskirts of Perranporth where Winston Graham himself lived, a stretch of coast now occupied by seaside houses. For the filming of the television series, several buildings were used – both a long way from Perranporth.

One building was Pendeen Manor Farm, not far from St Just-in-Penwith, but the most familiar building is probably Botallack Manor Farm, the fine granite farmhouse a mile further down the road. The building is mainly fifteenth century and its porch is made from two mighty blocks of granite. Neither of these buildings is open to the public, but the latter can be seen from the track leading down from Botallack to some of the finest cliff scenery in Cornwall.

Botallack was one of Cornwall's busiest mining areas, and the cliffs are dotted with old mine buildings and riddled with old mine shafts. The engine houses of the old Crown Mine are perched dramatically on the cliff edge, just above the reach of the sea. Its shaft sloped down to run out under the sea and on a stormy night miners could hear the sound of the waves crashing above them. Several scenes in *Poldark* were filmed along this stretch of coast, and anyone in search of the true spirit of Poldark's Cornwall is recommended to visit Botallack and walk along the coastal footpath in either direction.

For the second *Poldark* series, the BBC TV film crew also used a seventeenth century farmhouse and buildings near Portquin, not far from Port Isaac, to represent Nampara. This is also a working farm and not open to the public, but it can be seen distantly from the road leading down to the cove. The narrow inlet of Portquin itself was used for location filming, one of its small fisherman's cottages representing the home of Captain Blamey. Above the inlet rises Doyden Point, on which stands a quaint Regency Gothic folly, now owned by the National Trust, and familiar to *Poldark* viewers as the home of Dr Dwight Enys. Several scenes were filmed on this high headland.

Trenwith, the family home of the Poldarks and later of Elizabeth and George Warleggan, was partly based by Winston Graham on Trerice Manor, not far from Newquay. This fine Elizabethan house is also now owned by the National Trust and is open to the public. Its compact courtyard, gallery and great hall with its massive window will be familiar to *Poldark* readers but viewers will have to travel to Godolphin Hall, northwest of Helston, to find the building which represented Trenwith in the television series. Near the village of Townshend, this sixteenth century mansion, once the home of the Royalist Earls of Godolphin, is open to the public on some days during the summer months.

During the filming of the first *Poldark* series, it was decided to depart from the original plot and to burn down Trenwith in the final episode. So when the second series was made, it was therefore necessary to create a 'new' house, Penrice. For this, Boconnoc House near Lostwithiel, was chosen. Surrounded by a large wooded estate and deer park, it was a perfect location, and many scenes were shot in the grounds of this private 8,000-acre estate. The house is not open to the public except for charitable events in late April and May each year, and it was on one such occasion that the

Film 'extras' take a meal break at Portquin during work on the 'Poldark' series.

Elizabeth Poldark (Jill Townsend) might look an unlikely cricketer but her bowling saved the Poldark team from defeat in their charity match against the Warleggans at Boconnoc during a light-hearted break from filming.

'Poldark' creator Winston Graham *(right)* **looks on as the BBC film unit records the wedding of Caroline Penvenen and Dwight Enys at St Winnow Church on the banks of the Fowey.**

old rivalry between the Poldarks and the Warleggans came to a head – in a cricket match.

Thousands of fans turned up to watch as the evil George Warleggan (Ralph Bates), egged on by his motley team dressed in assorted tricorn hats, did his best to defeat his old rival. But all ended happily when, aided by some brilliant underarm bowling from Demelza (Angharad Rees), Ross Poldark (Robin Ellis) led his side to victory.

Not far from Boconnoc, and on the east bank of the River Fowey, is the grey granite church of St Winnow, the idyllic setting for the filming of the wedding of Dr Dwight Enys and Caroline Penvenen.

The tarmac path was covered with peat and electric lights on the wall of the church were shrouded with shrubbery, otherwise, there was no call for any further 'dressing'. The only problems here were caused by trains hauling china-clay along the railway line on the opposite bank just as the camera was about to roll, and the occasional low-flying jet. As the sound engineer said:

"Noise from jets is something we dread and just have to live with.

Otherwise, the atmosphere during filming could not have been happier even if the wedding had been 'for real'.

Other locations used by the *Poldark* film crew – apart from those mentioned earlier in this book – include St Enodoc Church and Towednack Church. The former, on the east bank of the River Camel and in the heart of Betjeman Country, was the setting for a wedding, as was the equally tiny church at Towednack, south west of St Ives.

The dungeons of St Mawes Castle, at the entrance to Carrick Roads, were used to represent a French prison in the second

The squat-towered church at Towednack, south west of St Ives, the setting for another of the 'Poldark' weddings.

Botallack Manor Farm, in West Cornwall, familiar to 'Poldark' viewers as the house 'Nampara' and to 'Penmarric' fans, as 'Roslyn'.

series. Visitors to the castle during filming were stunned to find the dark rooms lit by flickering brands and the floor covered with straw on which sprawled the lifeless bodies of uniformed prisoners. They were actually dummy figures, assembled in horrific poses. When filming the castle's exterior, several oil tankers sailed into view. But these were quickly transformed into galleons by being over-painted on a glass sheet in front of the camera.

The *Poldark* books of Winston Graham have given enormous pleasure to countless readers and television viewers, and, along with Daphne du Maurier, he is owed a large debt by all those who love Cornwall for his accurate portrayal of its past – the good times and the hard times.

The House of Penmarric

NO sooner had the BBC film crew finished filming *Poldark* than the location scouts were back in Cornwall, looking for suitable settings to film the *Penmarric* series.

Set in the St Just-in-Penwith area, Susan Howatch's story covers the years from 1867 to 1940, chronicling the fate and fortunes of one family. The family house of Penmarric, set in the heart of a tin-mining area, provides the backcloth for the saga.

Not surprisingly, the film makers, already familiar with this area from their *Poldark* days, decided to use many of the same locations, and for the farmhouse of Roslyn, they used the same farmhouse at Botallack they had used as Nampara.

A few miles north of Botallack is Levant Mine, scene of the terrible disaster in 1919 when the 'man-engine', a wooden beam used for lowering and raising miners, crashed down the shaft killing 31 men. Most of the mining sequences at the fictional Sennen Garth mine were filmed at Levant, which is still a working mine. Production assistant, Tony Garrick, explained difficulties involved:

'We had to virtually completely reconstruct a period mine and "dress" the existing master buildings to look authentic. The count house and offices that appeared on television were in fact entirely built in London, brought down to Levant and erected on the spot.

'Many of the moorland scenes of coaches diving along tracks were also filmed in this area and up on the Penwith moors. There are some marvellous old tracks and earth roads in Cornwall, just right for period filming. They hardly need anything adding or covering up.'

The tiny coastal village of Zennor with its church and pub, The

Set in the boulder-strewn landscape of the north Penwith coast is Zennor, the scene of filming for the 'Penmarric' series.

Tinners Arms, was used for several scenes in *Penmarric*, as was the magnificent cliff scenery at nearby Zennor Head and Cape Cornwall.

The beautiful gardens and house of Trengwainton, west of Penzance and once the home of the Arundell family, appeared in several episodes as Polzilliom. The front of the house was used for a wedding scene; the sub-tropical gardens with their towering ferns also provided a lush setting for several scenes.

For the house of Penmarric itself, the BBC diverged from the original book and took the film crew across the Tamar to Flete

House in Devon. I asked one technician how, in several scenes, Flete House was seen in a Cornish setting, with the sea in the background. He explained that a detailed image of the house was painted on a glass sheet and placed in front of the camera with the 'real' Cornish landscape behind. This method was also used to cover up unwanted buildings and pylons in many scenes.

'That forest you see on a skyline is probably only inches from the camera and could be masking a power-station or a housing estate,' he told me.

Certainly nothing is ever quite what it seems in the world of film and television. Even in Cornwall, where the lack of Urban sprawl and the availability of unspoilt villages allows the filming of period scenes without too much dressing of the location, things are changing. The growth of new industries and the need for new housing and better roads are all very necessary if Cornwall is to avoid stagnation. Heaven forbid that Cornwall's only attribute is its use as a film set museum. Like any other part of Britain, it has to move forward. But in Cornwall, more than most parts of the country, great care is needed to ensure that any development is achieved with acute sensitivity to location and landscape.

Large tracts of Cornwall remain relatively unspoilt – long may they remain so. And long may the cameras roll to record Cornwall's unique beauty.

The ruined engine-house of Crown Mine, perched on the cliff edge at Botallack, which was often featured in the 'Poldark' programmes.

Other Bossiney titles include ...

THE CRUEL CORNISH SEA
by David Mudd, 65 photographs.
David Mudd selects more than 30 Cornish shipwrecks, spanning 400 years, in his fascinating account of seas at a coastline that each year claim their toll of human lives.
'This is an important book.'
Lord St Levan, The Cornish Times

KING ARTHUR COUNTRY in CORNWALL
THE SEARCH for the REAL ARTHUR
by Brenda Duxbury, Michael Williams and Colin Wilson.
Over 50 photographs and 3 maps.
An exciting exploration of the Arthurian sites in Cornwall and Scilly, including the related legends of Tristan and Iseult, with The Search for the Real Arthur by Colin Wilson.
'... provides a refreshing slant on an old story linking it with the present.'
Caroline Righton, The Packet Newspapers

POLDARK COUNTRY
by David Clarke, 85 photographs.
The story behind the popular BBC TV series, including interviews with the cast and author Winston Graham.
'A fascinating insight into Cornwall and film making.'
BBC Radio

STRANGE HAPPENINGS IN CORNWALL
by Michael Williams, 35 photographs.
Strange shapes and strange characters; healing and life after death; reincarnation and Spiritualism; murders and mysteries are only some of the contents in this fascinating book.
'... this eerie Cornish collection.'
David Foot, Western Daily Express

We shall be pleased to send you our catalogue giving full details of our growing list of titles for Devon, Cornwall, Somerset, Dorset and Wiltshire as well as forthcoming publications. If you have difficulty in obtaining our titles, write direct to Bossiney Books, Land's End, St Teath, Bodmin, Cornwall.